Beginners Sneaker Hustle

The Ultimate Guide to Collecting, Buying, and Selling Sneakers

BY J.G. OJEDA

Copyright 2024 Beginner Sneaker Hustle by Author JG Ojeda

All rights reserved.

No portion of this book may be reproduced in any form without written permission from the author, except as pesrmitted by U.S. copyright law.

CONTENTS

Introduction 1
BEGINNER SNEAKER HUSTLE

Chapter 1 3
THE SNEAKER CULTURE REVOLUTION

Chapter 2 9
BUILDING YOUR SNEAKER KNOWLEDGE

Chapter 3 15
THE ART OF SNEAKER COLLECTING

Chapter 4 21
SNEAKER BUYING STRATEGIES

Chapter 5 27
SELLING SNEAKERS FOR PROFIT

Chapter 6 35
UNDERSTANDING SNEAKER CULTURE

Chapter 7 41
SNEAKER MAINTENANCE AND PRESERVATION

Chapter 8 47
SNEAKER TRADING AND NETWORKING

Chapter 9 .... **53**
BUILDING A SNEAKER RESELLING BUSINESS

Chapter 10 .... **59**
SNEAKER TECHNOLOGY AND INNOVATION

Chapter 11 .... **65**
SNEAKER CULTURE AND ITS IMPACT ON
FASHION AND SOCIETY

Chapter 12 .... **71**
SNEAKER AUCTIONS AND RARE RELEASES

INTRODUCTION
BEGINNER SNEAKER HUSTLE

by JG Ojeda

Welcome to *Beginner Sneaker Hustle*, your guide to entering the dynamic world of sneaker collecting, buying, and selling. Whether you're a passionate sneakerhead or someone looking to turn a love for kicks into a profitable side hustle, this book is for you. The sneaker market is booming, and the opportunities are endless if you know where to look and how to navigate the scene.

This book will take you through the essentials: from understanding sneaker culture to mastering the art of sourcing, negotiating, and flipping sneakers for profit. You don't need a fortune to start; just a keen eye, some hustle, and a willingness to learn.

Each chapter is packed with tips, tricks, and strategies designed to help you make smart decisions in this highly competitive, ever-evolving marketplace. By the end of *Beginner Sneaker Hustle*, you'll have the tools you need to start building your collection, finding deals, and making your mark in the sneaker world.

Let's lace up and step into the hustle!

CHAPTER 1
The Sneaker Culture Revolution

The Global Sneaker Phenomenon

Sneakers have become much more than simple footwear; they are symbols of status, culture, and personal style. What began as shoes made for athletes has evolved into a multi-billion-dollar industry that influences fashion, music, and even art. Today, sneakers hold a unique place in popular culture, with millions of people across the world collecting and wearing them. This chapter looks at how sneakers transformed from functional sportswear to cultural icons, setting the foundation for the world of sneaker collecting, buying, and selling.

The Early Days: Sneakers as Sportswear

The story of sneakers starts with sports. In the early 20th century, brands like Converse and Adidas began designing shoes specifically for athletes. Converse, for example, created the Chuck Taylor All-Star in 1917, a shoe that became popular with basketball players. Similarly, Adidas designed some of the first soccer cleats. Back then, sneakers were worn mostly for

Chapter 1

practical reasons — they offered athletes support, comfort, and performance on the court or field.

However, as more people saw athletes wearing these shoes, sneakers started to gain popularity beyond sports. By the 1950s and 1960s, sneakers were being worn casually, often as part of a rebellious style by teenagers and young adults. This shift set the stage for sneakers to enter mainstream culture.

The Rise of Sneaker Culture in the 1980s

The 1980s is when sneakers really started to take off, and there are two major reasons for this: Michael Jordan and hip-hop. In 1984, Nike partnered with NBA star Michael Jordan to create the Air Jordan 1. The shoes were revolutionary, not only because of their design but because of how Jordan played in them. People wanted to be like Mike, and wearing his shoes felt like a step toward that dream. The Air Jordan 1 didn't just change basketball — it changed the way people thought about sneakers. They became a status symbol, something cool to wear on and off the court.

At the same time, hip-hop was rising in popularity. Hip-hop artists, like Run-D.M.C., helped bring sneakers into the spotlight. In 1986, they released the song "My Adidas," which celebrated the sneakers they loved to wear. The group performed in Adidas Superstars, unlaced and with the tongues sticking out, creating a style that influenced a generation. This marked one of the first times that music and sneakers collided, and it was the start of a relationship that continues to this day.

The Golden Age of Sneakers: 1990s

If the 1980s laid the foundation, the 1990s were the golden age of sneaker culture. Sneakers became a full-blown phenomenon, driven by pop culture, sports, and the influence of technology. During this time, brands like Nike and Reebok pushed sneaker design to new levels. Nike introduced models like the Air Max, which featured visible air cushioning, and Reebok launched the Pump, a shoe that allowed wearers to inflate their sneakers for a custom fit.

Beyond the technical side, sneakers became a way for people to express their individuality. Skaters, rappers, and even movie stars embraced sneakers as part of their identity. Athletes continued to drive the popularity of sneakers, with players like Michael Jordan and Allen Iverson wearing signature models that became must-haves for sneakerheads. The 1990s also saw the release of some of the most iconic sneakers of all time, such as the Nike Air Max 95 and the Air Jordan 11.

The Sneakerhead Community: 2000s and Beyond

By the 2000s, sneakers had firmly established themselves as cultural icons, and a new group of enthusiasts emerged: sneakerheads. A sneakerhead is someone who collects, trades, and obsesses over sneakers, often spending hours hunting for rare or exclusive pairs. The internet played a huge role in building the sneakerhead community. Online forums like NikeTalk and websites like Sole Collector gave sneaker fans a place to share their collections, trade sneakers, and discuss upcoming releases.

One of the key developments during this time was the rise of limited sneaker releases, also known as "drops." Brands like Nike and Adidas began creating hype around certain sneakers by releasing them in small quantities, making them harder to get and, therefore, more desirable. This strategy worked perfectly, and it wasn't long before sneakerheads were lining up for hours, even days, to get their hands on a pair of exclusive sneakers.

The Role of Collaborations in Modern Sneaker Culture

Collaborations between sneaker brands and celebrities, artists, and designers have become a defining feature of modern sneaker culture. These collaborations often result in unique, limited-edition sneakers that blend fashion, art, and performance. One of the most famous examples is Kanye West's collaboration with Adidas to create the Yeezy line. The Yeezys were an instant hit, with pairs selling out in minutes and reselling for thousands of dollars.

Other major collaborations include Nike's work with designer Virgil Abloh, whose Off-White x Nike collection became one of the most sought-after sneaker lines in recent history. These partnerships between brands and influential figures have helped elevate sneakers to the level of high fashion, making them just as likely to be seen on a runway as on a basketball court.

The Future of Sneaker Culture

As sneaker culture continues to grow, new trends are emerging that will shape its future. One major trend is the focus on sustainability. Brands like Nike and Adidas are experimenting with eco-friendly materials, like recycled plastics and plant-based leathers, to create sneakers that have a lower environmental impact. Another trend is customization. Advances in technology, like 3D printing, are allowing sneakerheads to design and produce their own sneakers, giving them a level of control over their collections that was unheard of just a few years ago.

Sneaker culture is also becoming more global. While the U.S. remains a major player, sneaker culture is booming in countries like Japan, China, and Brazil. Thanks to social media, trends can spread across the world instantly, connecting sneakerheads in ways that were impossible before.

More Than Just Shoes

Sneakers are far more than just functional shoes. They represent culture, art, and even identity. Whether it's Michael Jordan's Air Jordans, Kanye West's Yeezys, or Virgil Abloh's Off-White collection, sneakers are woven into the fabric of modern culture.

As you continue reading this book, you'll not only learn about the history of sneakers, but also how to build, buy, sell, and maintain your own collection.

CHAPTER 2
Building Your Sneaker Knowledge

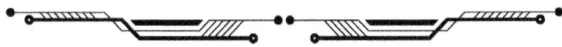

Why Knowledge Matters

To get into the sneaker game, whether you're collecting for fun or selling for profit, knowledge is your greatest tool. Understanding the culture, the language, and the history behind sneakers will make you better equipped to find the right pairs, make smart investments, and avoid costly mistakes. Sneaker culture has its own unique terms and rules, and without knowing them, it's easy to get lost. This chapter will lay the foundation you need to confidently navigate the world of sneakers.

Sneaker Terminology 101

Just like any hobby or industry, sneakers have their own vocabulary. Understanding these key terms will help you when buying, selling, and talking to other sneaker enthusiasts.

- Deadstock (DS): This means that a pair of sneakers has never been worn or even tried on. They are brand new, straight out of the box, and this condition is highly valued by collectors. Many people look for deadstock sneakers because they want shoes that are in mint condition.

- OG (Original): Refers to the first release of a particular sneaker model or colorway. If someone says they have an "OG pair," it means they own the original version of the shoe, not a retro or re-release.

- Retro: A re-release of a previously discontinued sneaker model. For example, Jordan Brand often retroes old models, bringing them back in new colorways or even their original colors.

- Hypebeast: This term is used to describe someone who buys sneakers (or other fashion items) solely for the hype or to follow trends. Hypebeasts often seek out popular or limited-edition items to show off.

- General Release (GR): Sneakers that are widely available and produced in large quantities. These shoes are easier to buy and usually don't sell out immediately, unlike limited-edition drops.

Knowing these terms helps you understand what you're looking for and communicate more easily with other collectors.

Major Sneaker Brands and Their Key Models

There are many brands in the sneaker world, but a few have risen to the top as the most influential. Let's look at some of the key players and their most iconic models:

- Nike: The global giant of the sneaker world, Nike's dominance is undeniable. The brand is known for its innovation in both technology and design. Some of the most famous models include the Air Jordan line, Air Max, and Nike Dunk. Nike's partnerships with athletes and designers have kept the brand at the forefront of sneaker culture.

- Adidas: Adidas is known for its Boost technology, which offers incredible comfort, and for its fashion-forward collaborations. Kanye West's Yeezy line has helped make Adidas a major player in the high-end sneaker game, while its NMD and Ultraboost models continue to be popular.

- Jordan Brand: While Jordan Brand is technically part of Nike, it has its own dedicated following. The Air Jordan line revolutionized sneaker culture in the 1980s, and today, Air Jordans remain some of the most coveted sneakers on the market.

- New Balance: New Balance has gained popularity recently, especially in the world of collaborations. Known for its comfortable shoes and quality craftsmanship, the brand has released limited editions with designers like Joe Freshgoods that have put them back on the sneaker map.

- Puma: Once considered more of a retro brand, Puma has made a comeback in recent years thanks to collaborations with fashion icons like Rihanna and Jay-Z. The Puma Suede, in particular, is an iconic model with deep roots in hip-hop culture.

Familiarizing yourself with these brands and their key models is the first step toward building a solid sneaker collection.

The Importance of Sneaker Collaborations

Collaborations have become a major driving force in sneaker culture. When a brand teams up with a designer, artist, or celebrity, the result is often a limited-edition sneaker that generates huge buzz.

One of the most famous collaborations is Kanye West's Yeezy line with Adidas. When the Yeezy Boost 350 first dropped, it sold out within minutes and became one of the most sought-after sneakers in the world. Another iconic collaboration is Virgil Abloh's Off-White x Nike collection, which reimagined classic Nike models with a deconstructed, industrial design. These types of collaborations not only increase the value of the sneakers but also create an emotional connection for fans of the artist or designer.

Sneaker Releases and Drops

Knowing how sneaker releases work is crucial if you want to collect or resell sneakers. Brands often create hype around specific sneakers by limiting their availability, making it harder to get a pair. This exclusivity can drive up demand and value.

- General Release (GR): These sneakers are widely available in stores and online, with no restrictions. General release sneakers are easier to get, and they don't usually sell out immediately.

- Limited Edition: Limited-edition sneakers are produced in smaller quantities, often as part of a collaboration or special event. These drops generate more excitement because of their rarity.

- Raffles: Raffles are a common way for brands and retailers to handle high-demand releases. People enter a raffle online or in-store, and winners are randomly selected to purchase the shoes. Raffles help manage the massive demand for exclusive sneakers.

- Shock Drops: Shock drops are unexpected releases where a sneaker is made available without any prior announcement. This tactic builds buzz and excitement as fans scramble to buy the sneakers before they sell out.

Understanding the different types of releases can help you prepare for drops and increase your chances of securing a pair of limited-edition sneakers. Go to the shoe name brand sites, subscribe to them, many time they text or email special early releases drops and other events.

Identifying Authenticity

Unfortunately, the sneaker industry is flooded with counterfeit products. As a collector or reseller, it's important to be able to identify fake sneakers to avoid losing money. Here are some tips for verifying authenticity:

- Packaging: Legitimate sneakers usually come in high-quality boxes with specific branding and labels. Pay attention to the details of the packaging, including the box design and any included accessories like extra laces or tissue paper.

- Stitching: Authentic sneakers have consistent, clean stitching, whereas counterfeit pairs often have crooked or uneven stitching.

- Tags and Labels: Authentic sneakers come with labels that display the correct font, size, and SKU (Stock Keeping Unit) number. Compare the tags and labels on the box with those on the sneakers themselves to ensure they match.

Knowing how to identify authentic sneakers will save you time and money, especially when purchasing from resale platforms or secondhand sellers.

Knowledge is Power

In the world of sneakers, knowledge truly is power. The more you know about the terminology, brands, releases, and how to spot authentic sneakers, the better prepared you are to succeed. Whether you're collecting for fun or selling for profit, understanding the basics will give you a strong foundation as you navigate the sneaker game. In the next chapter, we'll dive deeper into sneaker collecting and how to build a collection that reflects your personal style.

CHAPTER 3
The Art of Sneaker Collecting

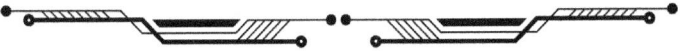

Why Collecting Sneakers is More Than a Hobby

Sneaker collecting has grown into a passion for millions of people worldwide, and for many, it's more than just a hobby — it's an art form. Whether you're a casual enthusiast or a serious collector, understanding the mindset behind collecting is essential. This chapter will guide you through the basics of sneaker collecting, from setting goals to maintaining your collection.

Defining Your Purpose as a Sneaker Collector

Every collector starts with a purpose, and defining yours early on will help you make smarter decisions. Are you collecting for personal enjoyment, investment, or nostalgia? Perhaps it's a combination of all three.

Some collectors focus on gathering sneakers from a specific era, such as the 1990s or early 2000s. Others focus on collecting a particular brand or model, such as Air Jordans or Nike SB Dunks. There's also the thrill of owning rare or limited-edition sneakers that hold significant value in the resale market.

Ask yourself:

- **Do you want to focus on specific models or colorways?**
- **Are you collecting for personal style or investment?**

- Do you have a budget or specific goals for your collection?

Your purpose will shape the direction of your collection and help you stay focused when making purchases.

Starting Small: Building Your Collection Over Time

While it might be tempting to dive in and buy the most hyped sneakers right away, it's better to start small and build your collection gradually. Begin by purchasing sneakers that you personally like or that have sentimental value to you. Not every sneaker in your collection needs to be rare or expensive. Some of the most meaningful collections are built from a mix of limited-edition and general-release sneakers.

A few tips for starting small:

- **Focus on quality, not quantity.** It's better to have a small collection of sneakers you love than a large one filled with pairs you rarely wear or don't care about.
- **Buy within your budget.** Don't stretch yourself too thin financially just to chase the latest release.
- **Rotate your collection.** As your tastes evolve, you might sell or trade sneakers to make room for new additions.

Starting small also gives you the chance to learn the ins and outs of sneaker releases, pricing, and resale value without feeling overwhelmed.

Choosing the Right Sneakers for Your Collection

Choosing which sneakers to add to your collection can be overwhelming, especially with so many options. One strategy is to focus on specific themes or goals for your collection. Some sneakerheads focus on collecting sneakers that represent significant moments in sports or pop culture. Others look for sneakers that feature unique collaborations or limited colorways.

Here are a few popular types of collections:

- **Signature Collections:** These focus on a single athlete, like collecting all Air Jordans or LeBron James' signature sneakers.

- **Collaboration Collections:** If you love fashion and design, collecting collaboration sneakers from brands like Nike, Adidas, and Puma might appeal to you. Iconic collaborations include Off-White x Nike, Yeezy x Adidas, and Travis Scott x Nike.

- **Nostalgia Collections:** Some collectors enjoy gathering sneakers they admired growing up or shoes that hold personal meaning, like their first pair of basketball sneakers.

Another important consideration is whether you want to keep sneakers deadstock (unworn) or wear them. While deadstock sneakers hold more resale value, some collectors enjoy actually wearing their sneakers as part of their personal style. One great example of how you can start off small, hit the thrift stores or online thrift shopping can land you some sweet deals. ShopGoodwill has a great online auction with loads of sneakers, we have found some awesome deals there. Just make sure to check the shipping when purchasing online.

Researching Sneaker Releases and Market Trends

Knowledge is power when it comes to sneaker collecting. The sneaker market can be unpredictable, with certain pairs gaining value over time while others lose it. Researching sneakers before making a purchase is crucial to making smart investments and finding sneakers that match your goals.

Key research areas include:

- **Release dates:** Knowing when new sneakers are dropping gives you a better chance of securing a pair at retail price before resellers drive up the cost.

- **Brand partnerships and collaborations:** Sneakers tied to big names in music, fashion, or sports often become valuable collector's items.

- **Historical value:** Sneakers tied to historic moments, such as Michael Jordan's first NBA championship or Kanye West's Grammy performance, often hold lasting value.

Staying up-to-date with sneaker blogs, YouTube channels, and social media accounts dedicated to sneaker culture can help you stay informed about upcoming releases and trends in the market.

The Value of Limited-Edition and Rare Sneakers

Limited-edition and rare sneakers are often the crown jewels of any collection. These sneakers are produced in small quantities, making them highly sought after by collectors and resellers alike. While not every limited-edition release will increase in value, the most coveted ones tend to appreciate over time.

Examples of rare sneaker categories include:

- **Player Exclusives (PEs):** Sneakers made specifically for athletes and not released to the public.

- **Friends and Family Releases:** Sneakers given to a brand's close associates or collaborators that are not available for retail purchase.

- **Sample Pairs:** Pre-production sneakers that are created in limited numbers to test designs before mass production.

Collecting rare sneakers can be expensive, so it's important to do thorough research and be patient. Keep an eye on secondary markets like StockX, GOAT, and eBay for opportunities to acquire rare pairs.

Storing and Maintaining Your Collection

Proper storage and maintenance are essential to keeping your sneaker collection in top condition. Sneakers, especially older or deadstock pairs, can degrade over time if not cared for properly. Whether you're displaying your collection or storing them long-term, here are some best practices to keep in mind:

- **Store in a cool, dry place.** Avoid exposure to direct sunlight, which can cause colors to fade and materials to break down. High humidity can also damage certain materials, such as leather and suede.
- **Use silica gel packs.** These absorb moisture and help keep your sneakers dry.
- **Rotate your sneakers.** Wearing your sneakers occasionally can help prevent them from deteriorating due to lack of use. For deadstock pairs, gently handling and airing them out can help maintain their structure.

For serious collectors, sneaker display cases or dedicated storage solutions can help show off your prized possessions while protecting them from dust and wear.

Making Your Collection Reflect You

At its core, sneaker collecting is about expressing your identity and passion. Whether you collect for the love of the shoes, their cultural significance, or their financial value, every sneaker tells a story. Your collection should be a reflection of your tastes, goals, and experiences. As you build your collection, remember

Chapter 3

that it's not just about the shoes — it's about the memories, the thrill of the hunt, and the community you become part of.

In the next chapter, we'll explore the business side of sneakers, diving into how to buy and sell sneakers for profit while navigating the often-competitive resale market.

CHAPTER 4
SNEAKER BUYING STRATEGIES

The Art of Finding the Perfect Pair

When it comes to sneaker collecting, buying the right pair is half the battle. Whether you're after a rare release, a classic, or a general release sneaker, understanding how to effectively buy sneakers is crucial. This chapter will dive into strategies for purchasing sneakers, from retail drops to resell platforms, and provide tips on how to maximize your chances of scoring the sneakers you want.

Retail vs. Resale: Knowing Where to Buy

There are two main avenues for buying sneakers: retail and resale. Each comes with its own pros and cons, and knowing the differences is key to making informed purchases.

- **Retail:** This means buying sneakers directly from the brand or a retailer at their initial release price. While this is the most cost-effective option, it's often the hardest since limited-edition sneakers sell out quickly. Retail outlets include brand websites (e.g., Nike.com, Adidas.com), physical stores, and apps like the Nike SNKRS app or Adidas CONFIRMED.
    - **Pros:** Best price, brand new condition.
    - **Cons:** High competition for limited releases, may require entering raffles or waiting in long lines.

Chapter 4

- **Resale:** Buying sneakers from a reseller after they've sold out at retail. Resale platforms include websites like StockX, GOAT, and eBay, as well as local resellers or sneaker consignment shops.
    - **Pros:** Easier to find rare or sold-out sneakers, variety of conditions (new and used).
    - **Cons:** Higher prices, risk of fakes, and additional fees on some platforms.

Knowing when to go the retail route and when to buy on the resale market can save you time, money, and frustration. For limited releases, being prepared for resale is often the best strategy.

Strategies for Securing Sneakers at Retail

If you want to buy sneakers at retail price, especially for limited releases, you need to be prepared. Popular releases sell out within minutes, and there's often heavy competition. Here are some strategies to maximize your chances of securing sneakers at retail:

- **Raffles:** Many brands and retailers use raffle systems for their most hyped releases. You'll need to enter your information (and sometimes pay upfront) for a chance to win the opportunity to buy the sneakers. Entering multiple raffles at different retailers can increase your chances.
- **Bots and Manual Methods:** Some people use automated bots to purchase sneakers as soon as they drop, giving them an edge over manual buyers. However, brands are cracking down on bots, and for casual collectors, learning how to manually secure sneakers with speed and timing is key.

- **Sneaker Apps:** Apps like Nike SNKRS and Adidas CONFIRMED give you access to exclusive sneaker drops, often through raffles or first-come, first-serve releases. Make sure you're logged in and ready to go at drop time.

- **Local Retailers:** Don't underestimate local sneaker stores. While big retailers get the most attention, smaller stores may have fewer buyers, giving you a better shot at scoring sneakers at retail.

Preparation and timing are key. Set alarms for drop times, have your payment and shipping information ready, and act fast. Also keep in mind that making friends with employees at a local shoe store can have its advantages, information is key when new shoes drop or when trucks come in with new shoes. Make a friend and get the inside scoop.

Navigating the Resale Market

If you miss out on a retail release, don't worry the resale market offers another chance to get your hands on coveted sneakers. However, shopping in the resale market comes with risks, like overpaying or buying counterfeit shoes. Here's how to navigate the resale market safely and smartly:

- **Platforms to Use:** Reputable resale platforms include StockX, GOAT, Stadium Goods, and Flight Club, Poshmark. These platforms often authenticate sneakers to ensure they're not fakes, providing buyers with more peace of mind.

- **Pricing Research:** Before making a purchase, research how much a sneaker is selling for across multiple platforms. Prices can fluctuate, especially right after a release, so it's important to shop around and wait for the right time to buy.

- **Authentication:** If you're buying from a private seller (through eBay, Craigslist, or local resellers), always ask for proof of authenticity. This could include the original receipt, detailed photos of the shoes and packaging, and any tags or labels that came with the sneaker.

Navigating the resale sneaker market effectively requires patience and a sharp eye for deals and authenticity. First, it's important to research the market value of sneakers you're interested in. This helps you avoid overpaying and ensures you're getting a fair deal. Always verify the authenticity of the sneakers, as fakes are common. Trusted platforms like StockX, GOAT, or Grailed often provide authentication services. Be patient, as finding the right pair at a good price can take time. Lastly, pay attention to market trends, as prices can fluctuate based on demand.

Timing Your Purchases for Best Deals

Timing can be everything when it comes to getting the best deal on sneakers. If you're looking to buy sneakers on the resale market, knowing when to buy can save you hundreds of dollars.

- **Right After Release:** Sneakers often sell for the highest prices right after they release. Many resellers list their pairs immediately, knowing the demand is high. If you're eager to buy, expect to pay a premium.

- **Wait It Out:** Prices often drop a few weeks or months after the initial release, once the hype dies down and more pairs hit the market. If a pair isn't extremely rare or iconic, <u>waiting can pay off</u>.

- **Seasonal Discounts:** Major retailers often offer sales and discounts during holidays or at the end of seasons. While these deals may not apply to the most hyped releases, general release sneakers and older models often go on sale.

Patience can be a virtue in the sneaker game, especially if you're willing to wait for prices to drop on resale platforms. Again, it could be weeks or months but you can save a ton of money.

How to Avoid Buying Fake Sneakers

The counterfeit sneaker market has become more sophisticated, making it harder to spot fakes. However, knowing how to identify fake sneakers can save you from making a costly mistake.

Here are a few ways to ensure you're buying authentic sneakers:

- **Check the Seller's Reputation:** Whether buying from an individual seller or a resale platform, always check the seller's reviews, ratings, and feedback.

- **Compare with Authentic Pairs:** Use online resources to compare your sneaker's details with authentic versions. Pay attention to the stitching, logos, and materials. Fake sneakers often have small errors in font, spacing, or stitching.

- **Ask for Detailed Photos:** If buying online, always request detailed photos of the sneakers, including the box, tags, and close-ups of the shoes from multiple angles.

- **Use Trusted Authentication Services:** If you're buying from a platform that doesn't authenticate sneakers, you can use services like CheckCheck or Legit Grails to have your sneakers professionally verified.

Being cautious can prevent you from wasting money on counterfeit sneakers, especially when shopping on less regulated platforms.

Chapter 4

Building Relationships with Retailers and Resellers

Networking is an underrated part of the sneaker game. Building relationships with local retailers, sneaker store employees, and resellers can give you an edge in securing rare sneakers.

Here's how to build connections:

- **Be Loyal to Retailers:** Support your local sneaker shops by shopping regularly. Store employees often remember repeat customers and may give you a heads-up about upcoming releases or hold a pair for you.

- **Network with Resellers:** Some resellers have early access to sneakers or a wide network of contacts who can help you find hard-to-get pairs. Building a good relationship with a trusted reseller can make it easier to track down rare sneakers.

- **Engage with the Sneaker Community:** Whether online or in person, becoming active in the sneaker community (through forums, social media, or events) can help you build valuable connections.

Networking can give you access to insider information and help you stay ahead of the competition for the most hyped releases.

Mastering the Sneaker Buying Process

The world of sneaker buying is both exciting and competitive. Whether you're purchasing at retail or resale, preparation and strategy are key to finding the right pair at the right price. By understanding how to navigate both markets, spotting fakes, and building relationships, you'll improve your chances of landing the sneakers you want.

In the next chapter, we'll explore selling sneakers, from setting the right prices to finding buyers and maximizing your profits in the resale market.

CHAPTER 5
SELLING SNEAKERS FOR PROFIT

Turning Sneakers into Cash

Selling sneakers can be a lucrative business, especially if you know how to navigate the resale market effectively. Whether you're looking to turn a quick profit or build a long-term income stream, understanding the best practices for selling sneakers is crucial. We will guide you through the steps of selling sneakers, from pricing and listing to shipping and customer service. You might wonder, is there money to be made? How about growth in the industry?

In the United States, the sneaker resale value is $2 billion in 2019, taking up more than a third of the entire reselling market in North America. By the end of 2023, the United States raked in another $2 billion in revenue in the secondhand sneaker market. There is huge room for a person with knowledge of sneakers to make a lot of money starting out small scale.

Pricing Your Sneakers

One of the most important aspects of selling sneakers is setting the right price. Price too high, and you may scare away potential buyers; price too low, and you might not maximize your profit. Here's how to price your sneakers effectively:

- **Research Market Value:** Start by researching how much similar sneakers are selling fore on resale platforms like StockX, GOAT, Grailed, Stadium Goods and eBay. Look at recent sales and current listings to get a sense of the going rate.

Chapter 5

- **Condition Matters:** The condition of your sneakers (new, lightly worn, or heavily worn) will affect their price. New or deadstock sneakers generally fetch a higher price than used ones. Be honest about the condition when listing.

- **Factor in Fees:** Resale platforms charge fees for selling items, which can range from 5% to 20% of the sale price. Make sure to factor these fees into your pricing so that you still make a profit after they're deducted.

- **Consider Scarcity and Demand:** Limited-edition sneakers or those with high demand often command higher prices. If you have a particularly sought-after pair, you can price them higher based on their rarity and demand.

Effective pricing requires a balance between market research and understanding the specific value of your sneakers. Price what you can live with it selling for, never be the cheapest but when starting our you need to sell quick to get a feel for the selling process and get rating on the platform you sell on.

Choosing the Right Platform to Sell

There are various platforms for selling sneakers, each with its own advantages and disadvantages. Choosing the right one can impact how quickly and profitably you sell your sneakers. Here's a look at some popular options:

- **StockX:** Known for its transparent pricing and authentication services, StockX is a popular platform for selling high-demand sneakers. The site provides a marketplace where buyers place bids, and you can either accept or reject them.
    - **Pros:** Authenticity guarantee, large audience.

- o **Cons:** Fees can be high, and the platform primarily caters to high-demand sneakers.
- **GOAT:** GOAT offers both new and used sneaker listings, and it also includes a verification process for authenticity. The platform has a reputation for good customer service and a wide range of sneakers.
    - o **Pros:** Authenticity checks, variety of listings.
    - o **Cons:** Fees and shipping requirements, competition from other sellers.
- **eBay:** A well-established marketplace where you can auction sneakers or sell them at a fixed price. eBay provides a large audience but doesn't include a built-in authentication service, so buyers may be wary of fakes.
    - o **Pros:** Large audience, auction options.
    - o **Cons:** Higher risk of counterfeit concerns, fees.
- **WhatNot:** A newer live auction site. Sneaker dealers this is a great new platform.
    - o **Pros:** Large audience, lower fees.
    - o **Cons**: Higher risk of counterfeit concerns, fees
- **Local Resale:** Selling sneakers locally through social media platforms, sneaker groups, or consignment stores can be another option. Local sales often involve less fee but require more effort in finding buyers.
    - o **Pros:** No shipping, lower fees. Unlimited potential
    - o **Cons:** Limited audience, potential safety concerns.

Chapter 5

Choosing the right platform depends on your sneakers' value, your desired selling price, and your comfort level with the platform's fees and processes. There are many others like Stadium Goods, Grailed, Poshmark and the list goes on. I believe the best way to start is local, get some inventory and post on Facebooks Market Place. Free ads, local pickup so no need to shipping, it's a great way to get your feet wet. Taking payments is easy with apps like CashApp, Zelle, Squire and the list goes on, fees are low and makes for easy transactions.

Creating an Attractive Listing

An attractive and detailed listing can make the difference between a quick sale and a long wait. When creating a listing, focus on providing clear and accurate information to attract potential buyers.

- **High-Quality Photos:** Include multiple high-resolution images of the sneakers from different angles, including close-ups of the tags, stitching, and any flaws. Good photos help buyers see the condition of the sneakers and build trust.

- **Detailed Description:** Provide a thorough description of the sneakers, including the model, size, colorway, condition, and any unique features. Mention any original packaging or accessories included.

- **Honest Condition Report:** Be transparent about any wear, scuffs, or defects. Honesty about the condition helps avoid disputes and returns later on.

- **Competitive Pricing:** Set a price that reflects the sneakers' market value while also considering the platform's fees and your desired profit.

An attractive listing with accurate information helps build buyer confidence and can lead to faster sales.

Handling Shipping and Returns

Efficiently managing shipping and returns is essential for a smooth selling experience. Here are some tips to ensure that you handle these aspects professionally:

- **Packaging:** Use sturdy, clean packaging to protect the sneakers during transit. If possible, ship them in their original box. Proper packaging helps prevent damage and reduces the likelihood of returns.

- **Shipping Options:** Choose reliable shipping carriers and offer tracking to buyers. Providing tracking information helps keep both you and the buyer informed about the shipment's status.

- **Handling Returns:** Be clear about your return policy in your listing. Some platforms automatically handle returns, but if you're selling locally or through other channels, set clear terms for returns and refunds.

Effective shipping and return management ensure that buyers receive their sneakers in good condition and can help build a positive reputation as a seller.

Building a Positive Reputation

A positive reputation as a seller can lead to more sales and higher prices for your sneakers. Here's how to build and maintain a good reputation:

- **Communicate Promptly:** Respond to buyer inquiries and messages quickly. Good communication helps build trust and shows that you're a reliable seller.

- **Provide Accurate Listings:** Ensure that your listings are honest and detailed. Accurate descriptions and clear photos prevent misunderstandings and disputes.

- **Deliver as Promised:** Ship items promptly and as described. Meeting or exceeding buyer expectations can lead to positive reviews and repeat business.

- **Handle Disputes Professionally:** If issues arise, handle them professionally and courteously. Resolving disputes in a fair manner can help maintain a good reputation.

Building a strong reputation can lead to increased trust from buyers and better sales opportunities. Collect customer information, name, phone & email addresses. Ask what they are looking for in the future and size matters. You get a new product that's a size 10, bam! you can shoot them a email or text letting them know. Customers love to feel they are the most important person in the world, so a quick text tells them they are important and getting the inside scoop.

Avoiding Common Selling Mistakes

To maximize your success as a sneaker seller, it's important to avoid common mistakes that can lead to problems or lost profits.

- **Overpricing:** Setting prices too high can scare off potential buyers. Research market prices and be realistic about what you can get for your sneakers.

- **Ignoring Platform Fees:** Be aware of the fees associated with different resale platforms and factor them into your pricing. Neglecting these fees can eat into your profits.

- **Neglecting Authenticity:** Failing to provide proof of authenticity or selling counterfeit sneakers can lead to disputes, returns, and damage to your reputation.

- **Poor Communication:** Not responding to buyer inquiries or failing to provide accurate information can lead to negative feedback and lost sales.

Avoiding these common pitfalls can help ensure a smoother selling experience and better results.

Mastering the Art of Selling Sneakers

Selling sneakers for profit involves a mix of strategy, research, and effective communication. By setting the right price, choosing the right platform, creating attractive listings, and managing shipping and returns, you can turn your sneakers into cash and build a successful resale business.

Next, we'll delve into the world of sneaker culture and the influence it has on collecting and reselling sneakers. Understanding the culture can enhance your approach and give you an edge in the market.

CHAPTER 6
Understanding Sneaker Culture

The Power of Sneaker Culture

Sneaker culture is more than just a trend; it's a global phenomenon that influences fashion, music, sports, and even social movements. Understanding sneaker culture can give you insights into why certain sneakers are so coveted and how they become cultural icons. This chapter will explore the roots of sneaker culture, its impact on various industries, and how it shapes the sneaker market.

The Origins of Sneaker Culture

Sneaker culture didn't happen overnight. It's the result of a blend of fashion, sports, and street culture that has evolved over decades. Here's a brief look at how sneaker culture began:

- **Early Influences:** Sneakers first gained prominence in the 20th century, with brands like Converse and Adidas leading the way. Converse's Chuck Taylor All-Stars became popular in the 1920s and 1930s, especially in basketball. In the 1970s and 1980s, brands like Nike and Adidas introduced new technologies and designs that set the stage for modern sneaker culture.

- **The Hip-Hop Era:** In the 1980s, hip-hop culture played a major role in popularizing sneakers. Artists like Run-D.M.C. and LL Cool J began wearing sneakers in their music videos and performances, elevating them to a status symbol in the urban community.

- **The Rise of Sports Endorsements:** The endorsement of athletes, notably Michael Jordan with Nike's Air Jordan line, revolutionized sneaker culture. Jordan's success and charisma helped turn sneakers into more than just sportswear; they became a symbol of style and success.

Understanding these origins helps explain why certain sneakers are considered iconic and how their cultural significance extends beyond mere fashion.

The Role of Sneaker Collaborations

Collaborations between sneaker brands and celebrities, designers, and artists have become a cornerstone of sneaker culture. These collaborations create limited-edition releases that often-become instant classics. Here's why they matter:

- **Celebrity Influence:** When celebrities endorse or collaborate on sneakers, they bring their personal brand and fan base to the product. Collaborations with figures like Kanye West (Yeezy) and Travis Scott (Nike) have created massive hype and demand.

- **Designer Touch:** Designers like Virgil Abloh (Off-White) and Hiroshi Fujiwara (Fragment Design) bring unique perspectives to sneaker design. Their limited-edition releases often become highly sought-after collector's items.

- **Cultural Impact:** Collaborations often tie in with broader cultural themes or social issues, making the sneakers not just a product but a statement. For example, collaborations that support charitable causes or promote social justice issues resonate with buyers on a deeper level.

Collaborations amplify the cultural impact of sneakers and can turn them into coveted collectibles. Check out some of these numbers: In the secondary sneaker market, Nike x Off-White collabs generate an average of 296% premium when resold.

- At 112%, Adidas x Bape sneaker collaborations are the second most profitable.

- Nike's collaborations with Fear of God and Travis Scott register a 101% and 93% increase from its retail price when sold in the resale market.

- Meanwhile, the Yeezy and Pharell Williams silhouettes with Adidas accumulate 65% and 38% price premiums.

Sneaker Culture and Fashion Trends

Sneakers have evolved from functional sportswear to a key component of high fashion. The integration of sneakers into everyday fashion and luxury shows how influential they've become:

- **Streetwear:** Sneakers are a staple of streetwear, a fashion style that blends casual, athletic, and urban elements. Brands like Supreme and Off-White have played a major role in elevating sneakers from the streets to high fashion.

- **Runway Shows:** High-fashion designers and luxury brands now frequently feature sneakers in their collections. This crossover from sportswear to luxury fashion shows how sneakers have become a versatile and essential part of modern style.

- **Sustainable Fashion:** Recently, there's been a growing trend towards sustainable fashion, including eco-friendly sneakers made from recycled materials. This shift reflects a broader concern for environmental issues within sneaker culture.

Chapter 6

Sneakers are no longer just for sports or casual wear; they've become a significant fashion statement that bridges various style genres.

Sneaker Culture's Influence on Music and Media

Music and media have played a significant role in shaping and amplifying sneaker culture. Here's how they intersect:

- **Music Videos and Lyrics:** Sneakers frequently appear in music videos and lyrics, often serving as a symbol of status and style. Iconic music videos from artists like Kanye West and Drake often feature exclusive or custom-designed sneakers.

- **Social Media:** Platforms like Instagram and TikTok have become essential for sneaker culture, with influencers, celebrities, and sneakerheads showcasing their collections and engaging with fans. Social media amplifies sneaker trends and drives hype around new releases.

- **Movies and Documentaries:** Films and documentaries about sneakers, such as "The Last Dance" (focused on Michael Jordan) and "Sneakerheadz," highlight the cultural significance of sneakers and their impact on sports, fashion, and society.

Media and music continuously shape how sneakers are perceived and valued, contributing to their cultural significance.

The Sneakerhead Community

Sneakerheads are more than just collectors; they're passionate individuals who share a deep love for sneakers and sneaker culture. The community aspect of sneaker culture includes:

- **Sneaker Conventions:** Events like Sneaker Con and complexCon bring together sneaker enthusiasts, brands, and resellers. These conventions offer a space to buy, sell, and trade sneakers, and often feature panels, workshops, and exclusive releases.

- **Online Forums and Groups:** Online communities and forums, such as Reddit's r/sneakers and various Facebook groups, provide platforms for sneakerheads to discuss releases, share knowledge, and connect with like-minded individuals.

- **Local Meetups:** Many cities have local sneaker meetups where collectors and enthusiasts gather to show off their collections, discuss the latest trends, and make trades.

Being part of the sneakerhead community can enhance your understanding of sneaker culture and provide valuable networking opportunities.

The Future of Sneaker Culture

Sneaker culture is constantly evolving, influenced by technological advancements, changing fashion trends, and societal shifts. Here's a look at what the future might hold:

- **Technological Innovations:** Advances in sneaker technology, such as self-lacing systems and 3D-printed shoes, are likely to shape the future of sneaker design and functionality.

- **Cultural Shifts:** As sneaker culture continues to grow globally, it will likely incorporate more diverse influences and trends. The impact of different cultures on sneaker design and marketing will continue to expand.

- **Sustainability:** The trend towards sustainable and eco-friendly sneakers is expected to grow. Consumers and brands are increasingly focused on environmental impact, and this will likely continue to influence sneaker culture.

Chapter 6

The future of sneaker culture promises to be dynamic, with new innovations and cultural shifts shaping how sneakers are designed, marketed, and worn.

Embracing Sneaker Culture

Understanding sneaker culture enriches your appreciation of sneakers and their significance beyond just footwear. Whether you're a collector, reseller, or casual enthusiast, knowing the cultural context enhances your engagement with the sneaker world. Embrace the culture, stay informed, and connect with the community to fully appreciate the impact and evolution of sneakers.

In the next chapter, we'll explore sneaker maintenance and preservation, ensuring your collection stays in top condition and retains its value.

CHAPTER 7
Sneaker Maintenance and Preservation

Keeping Your Collection in Top Shape

Proper maintenance and preservation are essential for keeping your sneakers looking fresh and retaining their value. Whether you're a collector or simply want to extend the life of your favorite pairs, knowing how to care for your sneakers can make a significant difference. This chapter will guide you through best practices for cleaning, storing, and preserving your sneakers.

Cleaning Your Sneakers

Regular cleaning helps maintain the appearance and condition of your sneakers. Here's how to clean different types of sneakers effectively:

- **Canvas Sneakers:** Use a mild detergent mixed with warm water. Gently scrub with a soft brush or cloth. Rinse with clean water and let air dry. Avoid soaking them as it can weaken the canvas material.

- **Leather Sneakers:** Clean leather sneakers with a damp cloth to remove surface dirt. Use a leather cleaner and conditioner to maintain the leather's suppleness and shine. Avoid using too much water, as leather can get damaged.

Chapter 7

- **Suede Sneakers:** Brush suede sneakers with a suede brush to remove dirt. For stubborn stains, use a suede eraser or a mixture of white vinegar and water. Avoid getting suede too wet, as it can cause staining.

- **Mesh and Knit Sneakers:** For sneakers with mesh or knit uppers, use a gentle detergent and warm water. Clean with a soft brush or cloth, then rinse thoroughly. Air dry away from direct heat sources.

Regular cleaning not only keeps your sneakers looking good but also helps prevent long-term damage.

Dealing with Stains and Odors

Sneakers can easily pick up stains and odors, especially with regular wear. Here's how to tackle common issues:

- **Removing Stains:** For fabric stains, use a mixture of baking soda and water to gently scrub the affected area. For leather stains, a leather cleaner or specialized stain remover can help. Always test cleaning products on a small, inconspicuous area first.

- **Eliminating Odors:** To combat odors, use sneaker-specific deodorizers or make your own by placing baking soda inside the sneakers and letting it sit overnight. For persistent smells, consider using sneaker fresheners or activated charcoal inserts.

Addressing stains and odors promptly prevents them from becoming permanent and keeps your sneakers smelling fresh.

Storing Your Sneakers

Proper storage is crucial for preserving the shape and condition of your sneakers. Here are some tips for effective storage:

- **Use Shoe Trees:** Inserting shoe trees helps maintain the shape of your sneakers, preventing creases and distortions. Choose shoe trees that fit the size and shape of your sneakers.

- **Keep Them Dry:** Store sneakers in a cool, dry place away from direct sunlight. Excessive moisture can lead to mold and mildew, while sunlight can cause fading and deterioration.

- **Use Dust Bags:** For high-value or rarely worn sneakers, store them in dust bags or original boxes to protect them from dust and potential damage.

Proper storage helps extend the life of your sneakers and keeps them in optimal condition.

Protecting Your Sneakers

Taking steps to protect your sneakers can prevent damage from common hazards. Here's how to safeguard your collection:

- **Waterproofing:** Use a waterproof spray designed for sneakers to protect against water and stains. Reapply periodically, especially if you wear your sneakers in wet conditions.

- **Avoiding Heavy Use:** Reserve high-value or delicate sneakers for special occasions. Frequent wear can lead to quicker wear and tear, reducing their lifespan and value.

- **Regular Maintenance:** Perform regular checks for any signs of wear or damage. Addressing minor issues early can prevent more significant problems down the line.

Protecting your sneakers ensures they remain in excellent condition and continue to look and feel great.

Chapter 7

Repairing Minor Damage

Minor repairs can often restore your sneakers to their original condition. Here's how to handle common issues:

- **Loose Soles:** If the sole starts to come loose, use a sneaker glue or adhesive to reattach it. Clean both surfaces before applying the glue for the best results.

- **Frayed Laces:** Replace frayed or broken laces with new ones. Laces are relatively inexpensive and can significantly improve the appearance of your sneakers.

- **Scuffs and Scratches:** For minor scuffs on leather, use a leather conditioner or polish to blend them in. Suede scuffs can be brushed out with a suede brush or treated with a suede-specific repair kit.

Minor repairs can help you maintain the functionality and appearance of your sneakers without needing to replace them.

Long-Term Preservation for Collectors

For sneaker collectors, long-term preservation is key to maintaining value and condition. Here's how to care for collectible sneakers:

- **Climate Control:** Store collectible sneakers in a climate-controlled environment to prevent issues with temperature and humidity. Avoid basements or attics where conditions can fluctuate.

- **Display Cases:** Use display cases or glass cabinets to showcase your sneakers while protecting them from dust and environmental damage. UV-protective glass can also prevent fading from sunlight.

- **Professional Services:** Consider using professional sneaker restoration services for high-value or heavily worn sneakers. These services can offer specialized cleaning, repairs, and preservation techniques.

Long-term preservation helps ensure that collectible sneakers retain their value and remain in pristine condition.

Caring for Your Sneakers

Proper maintenance and preservation are essential for keeping your sneakers looking their best and extending their lifespan. Whether you're a casual wearer or a dedicated collector, following these tips will help you protect your investment and enjoy your sneakers for years to come.

In the next chapter, we'll explore the world of sneaker trading and networking, providing insights into how you can build connections and trade sneakers with other enthusiasts.

CHAPTER 8
Sneaker Trading and Networking

Building Connections in the Sneaker World

Sneaker trading and networking are crucial aspects of the sneaker culture, allowing enthusiasts to acquire rare pairs, expand their collections, and engage with the community. Building strong connections and understanding the dynamics of sneaker trading can enhance your experience and success in the sneaker world. This chapter will guide you through the essentials of sneaker trading and networking.

The Basics of Sneaker Trading

Sneaker trading involves exchanging sneakers with other collectors or resellers to acquire new pairs or fulfill specific needs. Here's how to get started:

- **Know Your Market:** Research the value and demand for the sneakers you want to trade. Use platforms like StockX and GOAT to check current market prices and trends.

- **Find Trading Partners:** Look for potential trading partners through sneaker forums, social media groups, and local sneaker events. Networking with other enthusiasts can help you find opportunities for trades.

- **Negotiate Fair Trades:** When proposing a trade, ensure that the value of the sneakers you're offering is

Chapter 8

comparable to those you're seeking. Be honest about the condition of your sneakers to avoid disputes.

Effective trading requires research, negotiation skills, and a clear understanding of the value of the sneakers involved.

Networking in the Sneaker Community

Networking is essential for building relationships and gaining access to exclusive sneaker releases and trade opportunities. Here's how to network effectively:

- **Join Sneaker Groups:** Become an active member of online sneaker communities, such as Reddit's r/sneakers or Facebook sneaker groups. Engage in discussions, share your knowledge, and build relationships with other members.

- **Attend Sneaker Events:** Participate in sneaker conventions, meetups, and launch events. These gatherings provide opportunities to connect with fellow enthusiasts, trade sneakers, and learn about upcoming releases.

- **Use Social Media:** Follow sneaker influencers, brands, and collectors on platforms like Instagram and Twitter. Engaging with their content and participating in discussions can help you stay updated on trends and network with key figures in the sneaker world.

Networking helps you stay connected with the community and opens doors to valuable trading opportunities.

Utilizing Sneaker Forums and Online Marketplaces

Sneaker forums and online marketplaces are valuable resources for trading and networking. Here's how to make the most of these platforms:

- **Sneaker Forums:** Sites like NikeTalk and Sneaker Freaker forums offer dedicated spaces for discussing sneaker releases, trades, and collecting. Participate in discussions, share your insights, and use the trading sections to find potential deals.

- **Online Marketplaces:** Platforms like eBay and Grailed have sections for trading and buying sneakers. Use these platforms to search for specific pairs, connect with sellers, and explore trading options.

- **Reputation and Reviews:** When trading or purchasing on online marketplaces, check the seller's reputation and reviews. This helps ensure that you're dealing with trustworthy individuals and reduces the risk of scams.

Online platforms provide a broad reach for trading and networking but require vigilance to ensure safe transactions.

Building and Maintaining Relationships

Strong relationships with other sneaker enthusiasts can lead to more successful trades and collaborations. Here's how to build and maintain these connections:

- **Be Reliable:** Follow through on promises and agreements. If you commit to a trade or transaction, make sure to complete it as agreed.

- **Communicate Clearly:** Maintain open and honest communication with your trading partners. Discuss any concerns or issues promptly to avoid misunderstandings.

- **Support Others:** Help fellow enthusiasts by sharing information, offering advice, or assisting with trades. Building a positive reputation as a supportive member of the community can lead to reciprocal benefits.

Maintaining good relationships within the sneaker community enhances your reputation and can lead to more opportunities.

Avoiding Common Trading Pitfalls

To ensure successful and fair trades, be aware of common pitfalls and how to avoid them:

- **Counterfeit Sneakers:** Verify the authenticity of sneakers before trading. Use authentication services or check for signs of counterfeit sneakers to avoid scams.

- **Misleading Information:** Be honest about the condition and value of the sneakers you're offering. Misleading information can lead to disputes and damage your reputation.

- **Shipping Issues:** When trading, use reliable shipping methods and track your packages to ensure they reach their destination. Disputes over shipping can be avoided by providing tracking information and timely updates.

Avoiding these pitfalls helps ensure smooth and successful trading experiences.

The Role of Sneaker Resellers

Sneaker resellers play a significant role in the sneaker market, often acquiring limited releases and selling them at a premium. Understanding the role of resellers can help you navigate the market more effectively:

- **Market Influence:** Resellers often drive up the prices of highly sought-after sneakers by buying them in bulk and selling them at higher prices. This can create challenges for collectors trying to buy at retail prices.

- **Resale Strategies:** Some resellers use strategies such as bot programs to secure limited releases. Knowing these strategies can help you understand market dynamics and plan your buying and trading approaches accordingly.

- **Ethical Considerations:** The ethics of sneaker reselling can be debated, as it can impact accessibility and affordability for collectors. Consider these factors when engaging with the resale market.

Understanding the role of resellers helps you navigate the sneaker market and make informed decisions.

Expanding Your Network

As you build your network, consider ways to expand and diversify your connections:

- **Collaborate with Influencers:** Partner with sneaker influencers or bloggers to gain visibility and connect with a wider audience. Collaborations can also lead to exclusive trade opportunities.

- **Engage with Local Communities:** Participate in local sneaker groups and events to connect with enthusiasts in your area. Building local relationships can lead to valuable trades and networking opportunities.

- **Stay Informed:** Keep up with industry news and trends to stay relevant and informed. Being knowledgeable about upcoming releases and market shifts helps you make better trading decisions.

Expanding your network enhances your opportunities and connections in the sneaker world.

Thriving in the Sneaker Community

Sneaker trading and networking are integral parts of the sneaker culture, providing opportunities to acquire rare pairs, connect with other enthusiasts, and enhance your overall experience. By

Chapter 8

understanding the basics of trading, effectively networking, and avoiding common pitfalls, you can navigate the sneaker world with confidence and success.

In the next chapter, we'll explore the business side of sneaker reselling, including strategies for building a reselling business and managing inventory.

CHAPTER 9
BUILDING A SNEAKER RESELLING BUSINESS

Turning Passion into Profit

Sneaker reselling can be more than a hobby; it can become a profitable business venture. Understanding the fundamentals of building and managing a sneaker reselling business is essential for turning your passion for sneakers into a successful enterprise. This chapter will guide you through the steps of starting, growing, and managing a sneaker reselling business.

Starting Your Reselling Business

Starting a sneaker reselling business involves several key steps:

- **Research and Planning:** Begin by researching the sneaker market, including trends, popular brands, and key players. Develop a business plan that outlines your goals, target market, and strategies for sourcing and selling sneakers. Remember: Fail to plan, plan to fail.

- **Legal Considerations:** Register your business and choose a legal structure (e.g., sole proprietorship, LLC). This step is important for handling taxes, liabilities, and formalizing your business operations. Starting small you can go get a D.B.A. at you local court and open a bank account with that name.

- **Funding:** Determine how much capital you need to start your business. This includes funds for purchasing inventory, marketing, and other operational expenses. Consider personal savings, loans, or investments as potential sources of funding.

Starting your reselling business with a solid plan and legal foundation sets the stage for long-term success.

Sourcing Inventory

Sourcing inventory is a crucial aspect of sneaker reselling. Here's how to find and acquire sneakers to resell:

- **Retail Releases:** Monitor retail websites, apps, and stores for new sneaker releases. Use tools and apps to track release dates and secure pairs as soon as they drop.

- **Online Marketplaces:** Platforms like eBay, Grailed, and StockX can be sources for acquiring sneakers to resell. Look for undervalued or rare pairs that you can purchase and resell at a higher price.

- **Sneaker Conventions:** Attend sneaker conventions and trade shows to find rare or exclusive pairs. Networking with other resellers and collectors can also provide opportunities to acquire inventory.

- **Local Deals:** Explore local opportunities by connecting with other collectors or checking local marketplaces for potential finds.

Effective sourcing ensures that you have a steady supply of valuable sneakers for your reselling business.

Pricing Strategies

Setting the right prices for your sneakers is crucial for maximizing profit and remaining competitive:

- **Market Research:** Use platforms like StockX and GOAT to research current market prices and trends. Pricing your sneakers competitively helps attract buyers and ensures profitability.

- **Cost Analysis:** Calculate the total cost of acquiring each pair, including purchase price, shipping, and any additional fees. Set your resale price to cover costs and achieve your desired profit margin.

- **Dynamic Pricing:** Adjust your pricing based on demand and market conditions. For highly sought-after sneakers, consider pricing higher to capitalize on increased demand.

Effective pricing strategies help you balance profitability with competitiveness in the sneaker market.

Marketing and Sales Channels

Marketing your reselling business and choosing the right sales channels are key to reaching potential buyers:

- **Online Storefront:** Create an online store or use established platforms like eBay, Grailed, and StockX to sell your sneakers. Having a professional-looking storefront enhances credibility and attracts buyers.

- **Social Media:** Utilize social media platforms like Instagram, Facebook, and Twitter to promote your sneakers and engage with potential customers. Share high-quality images, updates on new releases, and special offers to build your brand.

- **Advertising:** Consider investing in online advertising to reach a larger audience. Platforms like Google Ads and social media ads can target specific demographics and increase visibility.

Chapter 9

Effective marketing and choosing the right sales channels help you reach a broader audience and boost sales.

Managing Inventory

Proper inventory management is essential for running a successful reselling business:

- **Tracking Inventory:** Use inventory management software or spreadsheets to keep track of your stock levels, sales, and restocks. Accurate tracking helps prevent overstocking or running out of popular items.

- **Organizing Storage:** Store your sneakers in a clean, organized manner to prevent damage and make them easy to locate. Consider using shelving units, clear bins, or labeled boxes for efficient storage.

- **Monitoring Trends:** Stay updated on sneaker trends and adjust your inventory accordingly. This helps ensure that you're stocking items that are in demand and can generate sales.

Effective inventory management ensures that you maintain a well-organized stock and meet customer demands.

Handling Customer Service

Providing excellent customer service can set your reselling business apart and build a loyal customer base:

- **Clear Communication:** Communicate clearly and promptly with customers regarding their orders, shipping status, and any issues. Transparency helps build trust and improve customer satisfaction.

- **Handling Returns and Refunds:** Establish a clear policy for returns and refunds. Ensure that your process is fair and easy for customers to understand.

- **Building Relationships:** Engage with customers through follow-ups, personalized messages, and special offers. Building strong relationships can lead to repeat business and positive word-of-mouth.

Excellent customer service enhances your business's reputation and encourages repeat purchases.

Scaling Your Business

Once your reselling business is established, consider ways to scale and grow:

- **Expanding Inventory:** Increase the variety and quantity of sneakers you offer. This can involve diversifying into different brands or styles and expanding your sourcing channels.

- **Hiring Help:** As your business grows, consider hiring additional staff or outsourcing tasks such as customer service, shipping, or inventory management.

- **Exploring New Markets:** Look for opportunities to enter new markets or regions. Expanding your reach can help you tap into new customer bases and increase sales.

Scaling your business involves strategic planning and investment to achieve sustained growth and success.

Succeeding in Sneaker Reselling

Building a successful sneaker reselling business requires careful planning, effective sourcing, strategic pricing, and excellent customer service. By understanding the fundamentals of reselling, managing inventory, and scaling your operations, you can turn your passion for sneakers into a profitable business venture.

Chapter 9

In the next chapter, we'll explore the impact of sneaker technology and innovation, including advancements in sneaker design and how they influence the market.

CHAPTER 10
SNEAKER TECHNOLOGY AND INNOVATION

The Evolution of Sneaker Design

Sneaker technology and innovation have transformed the sneaker industry, pushing the boundaries of design, comfort, and performance. Understanding these advancements not only enhances your appreciation of sneakers but also helps you make informed decisions when buying or reselling. This chapter will explore key technological innovations in sneakers and their impact on the market.

Key Technological Advancements

Over the years, several key technologies have revolutionized sneaker design. Here's a look at some of the most significant innovations:

- **Air Cushioning:** Introduced by Nike in 1978, Air cushioning involves encapsulating air in a durable, flexible unit within the sole of the sneaker. This technology provides superior comfort and impact absorption. Models like the Nike Air Max are iconic examples of Air cushioning in action.

- **Boost Technology:** Developed by Adidas, Boost technology uses thermoplastic polyurethane (TPU) foam to deliver exceptional energy return and cushioning. The Adidas Ultra Boost is a popular example, known for its responsive and comfortable ride.

- **Flyknit and Primeknit:** Nike's Flyknit and Adidas' Primeknit technologies use advanced knitting techniques to create lightweight, breathable, and flexible upper materials. These innovations enhance comfort and performance while reducing waste in the manufacturing process.

- **Gore-Tex and Waterproofing:** Gore-Tex is a waterproof, breathable fabric used in sneakers to protect against water while allowing moisture to escape. This technology is ideal for outdoor or all-weather sneakers, ensuring dry and comfortable feet.

These technological advancements have improved the functionality and comfort of sneakers, influencing both consumer preferences and market trends.

The Impact on Sneaker Performance

Technological innovations significantly impact sneaker performance, affecting everything from comfort to durability:

- **Enhanced Comfort:** Technologies like Air cushioning and Boost provide superior comfort by reducing the impact on joints and enhancing overall cushioning. This makes sneakers more suitable for various activities, from running to everyday wear.

- **Improved Fit:** Flyknit and Primeknit technologies offer a custom-like fit by adapting to the shape of the foot. This enhances stability and reduces the risk of blisters or discomfort.

- **Durability:** Innovations in materials and construction methods improve the durability of sneakers. For example, advanced rubber compounds and reinforced stitching extend the lifespan of sneakers, making them more resistant to wear and tear.

Understanding how these technologies enhance performance can help you make informed choices when buying or reselling sneakers.

The Role of Innovation in Sneaker Design

Innovation drives sneaker design, leading to new aesthetics and functional features:

- **Design Trends:** Technology often influences design trends, such as the sleek, minimalistic look of Flyknit uppers or the bold, futuristic style of sneakers with visible Air cushioning. Staying updated on design trends helps you identify popular models and anticipate market demand.

- **Collaborations:** Many sneaker brands collaborate with designers, athletes, and influencers to create innovative and exclusive designs. These collaborations often result in limited-edition releases that attract significant attention from collectors and resellers.

- **Customization:** Advances in technology have led to customizable sneakers, allowing consumers to personalize colors, materials, and features. This trend caters to individual preferences and creates unique, one-of-a-kind designs.

Innovation in sneaker design enhances both aesthetics and functionality, influencing consumer preferences and market dynamics.

Sneaker Technology and Market Trends

Technological advancements impact market trends and consumer behavior:

- **Performance vs. Style:** While performance technologies cater to athletes and fitness enthusiasts, style-focused innovations appeal to fashion-conscious consumers. Understanding these preferences helps you target the right audience for your reselling business.

- **Limited Editions:** Sneakers featuring cutting-edge technology or exclusive designs often become highly sought after, leading to increased demand and resale value. Keeping an eye on these releases can provide valuable trading opportunities.

- **Sustainability:** Environmental concerns are driving innovations in sustainable materials and production methods. Sneakers made from recycled materials or designed to be more eco-friendly are gaining popularity and may become a significant trend in the market.

Being aware of how technology influences market trends helps you stay competitive and make informed decisions in the sneaker industry.

The Future of Sneaker Technology

The future of sneaker technology promises even more exciting advancements:

- **Smart Sneakers:** Innovations in smart technology may lead to sneakers with built-in sensors, tracking performance metrics, and providing real-time feedback. These features could revolutionize the way we interact with and use sneakers.

- **Advanced Materials:** Research into new materials, such as self-healing fabrics or 3D-printed components, could further enhance the performance, comfort, and durability of sneakers.

- **Sustainability Initiatives:** Continued focus on sustainability may lead to new eco-friendly technologies and practices, such as biodegradable materials or circular production models that reduce waste.

Staying informed about future developments in sneaker technology helps you anticipate trends and opportunities in the market.

Embracing Sneaker Innovation

Sneaker technology and innovation play a crucial role in shaping the sneaker industry, influencing design, performance, and market trends. By understanding these advancements, you can make more informed decisions when buying, reselling, or collecting sneakers. Embracing innovation not only enhances your appreciation of sneakers but also positions you to capitalize on emerging trends and opportunities.

In the next chapter, we'll delve into sneaker culture and its influence on fashion and society, exploring how sneakers have become a significant cultural phenomenon.

CHAPTER II
SNEAKER CULTURE AND ITS IMPACT ON FASHION AND SOCIETY

The Rise of Sneaker Culture

Sneaker culture has evolved from a niche interest into a major cultural and fashion phenomenon. Sneakers are no longer just athletic wear; they have become symbols of style, status, and self-expression. This chapter explores the roots of sneaker culture, its influence on fashion and society, and how it has become a global trend.

The Origins of Sneaker Culture

Sneaker culture began to take shape in the late 20th century, driven by several key factors:

- **Athletic Influence:** Sneakers gained prominence through their association with athletes and sports. Iconic figures like Michael Jordan and his Air Jordan line helped establish sneakers as symbols of performance and status.

- **Hip-Hop and Streetwear:** The rise of hip-hop culture in the 1980s and 1990s played a significant role in popularizing sneakers. Artists and musicians embraced sneakers as part of their style, influencing trends and making them central to streetwear fashion.

- **Collecting and Reselling:** The practice of collecting and reselling sneakers emerged as a way to acquire rare and limited-edition pairs. This aspect of sneaker culture has grown into a significant market, with enthusiasts and investors driving demand.

The origins of sneaker culture are rooted in sports, music, and the emerging trend of sneaker collecting, setting the stage for its widespread impact.

Sneaker Culture and Fashion

Sneaker culture has had a profound impact on fashion, reshaping trends and influencing design:

- **Streetwear Integration:** Sneakers have become a staple of streetwear fashion, complementing casual and urban styles. Brands like Supreme and Off-White have collaborated with sneaker companies to create high-profile releases that blend fashion and function.
- **High-Fashion Collaborations:** Luxury brands and designers have embraced sneakers, incorporating them into their collections. Collaborations between brands like Balenciaga and Adidas or Louis Vuitton and Nike have blurred the lines between high fashion and athletic wear.
- **Style Statements:** Sneakers are now seen as style statements rather than just functional footwear. Customization, limited editions, and unique designs allow individuals to express their personal style and make a statement.

The integration of sneakers into mainstream fashion highlights their significance as more than just athletic gear, reflecting broader cultural trends.

The Social Impact of Sneakers

Sneakers have made a significant impact on society, influencing various social aspects:

- **Status and Identity:** Sneakers often represent social status and identity, with limited-edition releases and designer collaborations signifying exclusivity and success. Owning rare or high-value sneakers can be a status symbol in certain communities.

- **Community and Identity:** Sneaker culture fosters a sense of community among enthusiasts and collectors. Events, forums, and social media platforms provide spaces for individuals to connect, share their passion, and build relationships.

- **Economic Impact:** The sneaker industry generates significant economic activity through retail, resale, and related sectors. Sneaker releases and collaborations can drive substantial revenue and influence market trends.

The social impact of sneakers extends beyond fashion, affecting identity, community, and the economy.

Sneaker Culture Around the World

Sneaker culture is a global phenomenon, with unique expressions and trends in different regions:

- **United States:** The U.S. is a major hub for sneaker culture, with cities like New York and Los Angeles serving as epicenters for sneaker releases and events. The influence of hip-hop and sports culture is particularly strong.

- **Japan:** Japan is known for its unique sneaker culture, characterized by a blend of high fashion, streetwear, and meticulous attention to detail. Japanese sneakerheads often focus on rare and collectible releases, with a strong emphasis on craftsmanship.

- **Europe:** Sneaker culture in Europe has seen significant growth, with cities like London and Paris becoming key

Chapter 11

players in the market. European sneaker enthusiasts often blend streetwear with high fashion, reflecting diverse influences and trends.

Understanding global variations in sneaker culture provides insight into its widespread influence and diverse expressions.

The Future of Sneaker Culture

Sneaker culture continues to evolve, with several trends shaping its future:

- **Sustainability:** Growing awareness of environmental issues is leading to a focus on sustainable practices in sneaker production. Brands are exploring eco-friendly materials and processes to meet consumer demand for greener products.

- **Technology Integration:** The integration of technology, such as smart sneakers and virtual reality experiences, is likely to influence the future of sneaker culture. Innovations in design and functionality will continue to drive trends.

- **Cultural Shifts:** As sneaker culture evolves, new cultural influences and trends will shape its future. The continued blending of fashion, technology, and social issues will play a role in defining the next phase of sneaker culture.

Anticipating future trends in sneaker culture helps you stay informed and adapt to emerging influences and opportunities.

Embracing Sneaker Culture

Sneaker culture has become a powerful force in fashion and society, shaping trends, influencing style, and creating communities. By understanding its origins, impact, and future, you can appreciate the broader significance of sneakers and their role in contemporary culture.

In the next chapter, we'll explore the world of sneaker auctions and rare releases, providing insights into how to navigate high-stakes sneaker transactions and acquire coveted pairs.

CHAPTER 12
SNEAKER AUCTIONS AND RARE RELEASES

Navigating High-Stakes Sneaker Transactions

Sneaker auctions and rare releases are the pinnacle of sneaker collecting, offering opportunities to acquire coveted pairs that are often sold at premium prices. Understanding how to navigate these high-stakes transactions can help you secure rare sneakers and maximize your investment. This chapter will guide you through the processes of participating in sneaker auctions, accessing rare releases, and managing high-value transactions.

Understanding Sneaker Auctions

Sneaker auctions are platforms where rare and limited-edition sneakers are sold to the highest bidder. Here's how to effectively participate in sneaker auctions:

- **Choose the Right Platform:** Several auction platforms specialize in sneakers, such as Sotheby's, Christie's, and specialized sneaker auction sites like Stadium Goods and GOAT. Research each platform's reputation, fees, and bidding processes.

- **Know the Auction Terms:** Understand the auction terms, including starting bids, reserve prices, and bidding increments. Familiarize yourself with the auction's rules and deadlines to avoid missing out on your desired pair.

- **Set a Budget:** Establish a budget before participating in an auction. Rare sneakers can command high prices, so it's important to set a limit and avoid getting caught up in bidding wars.

Effective participation in sneaker auctions requires research, preparation, and financial discipline to secure rare pairs without overextending your budget.

Accessing Rare Sneaker Releases

Rare sneaker releases are often highly sought after, and gaining access to them can be challenging. Here's how to improve your chances of securing rare releases:

- **Follow Release Calendars:** Stay updated on sneaker release calendars from brands, retailers, and sneaker news sites. Knowing release dates and times helps you plan and prepare for purchasing.

- **Use Sneaker Bots:** Sneaker bots are automated tools designed to increase your chances of securing limited releases by quickly navigating online stores. While effective, they can be costly and may violate some retailers' terms of service.

- **Participate in Raffles:** Many brands and retailers use raffles to distribute limited-edition sneakers. Enter as many raffles as possible to increase your chances of winning the opportunity to purchase rare pairs.

- **Join Sneaker Communities:** Engage with sneaker communities and forums where members share release information, tips, and opportunities. Networking with other enthusiasts can provide valuable insights and increase your chances of success.

Securing rare sneaker releases involves staying informed, using available tools, and actively participating in sneaker communities.

Managing High-Value Transactions

Handling high-value sneaker transactions requires careful management to ensure a smooth and secure process:

- **Verify Authenticity:** Ensure that the sneakers you're buying or selling are authentic. Use authentication services or seek expert opinions to verify the legitimacy of high-value pairs.

- **Secure Payment Methods:** Use secure payment methods, such as credit cards or trusted payment platforms, to protect against fraud. Avoid using cash or unverified payment methods for high-value transactions.

- **Arrange Safe Shipping:** When buying or selling high-value sneakers, use reliable shipping methods with tracking and insurance. Proper packaging and shipping ensure that the sneakers arrive in the expected condition.

Managing high-value transactions with attention to detail helps prevent issues and ensures a secure and satisfactory experience.

The Role of Sneaker Resale Marketplaces

Sneaker resale marketplaces are platforms where collectors and resellers buy and sell sneakers, often at a premium. Here's how to navigate these marketplaces:

- **Research Marketplaces:** Familiarize yourself with popular resale marketplaces such as StockX, GOAT, and Grailed. Each platform has its own policies, fees, and authentication processes.

- **Understand Market Value:** Research the current market value of the sneakers you're interested in buying or selling. Platforms like StockX provide price history and market trends to help you make informed decisions.

- **Build a Reputation:** As a seller on resale marketplaces, building a positive reputation through good customer service and accurate listings is crucial for success. Positive reviews and ratings can enhance your credibility and attract buyers.

Navigating resale marketplaces involves understanding platform specifics, researching market values, and maintaining a strong reputation as a seller.

Strategies for Selling Rare Sneakers

Selling rare sneakers requires strategic planning to achieve the best results:

- **Price Competitively:** Set a competitive price based on market research and the rarity of the sneakers. Be aware of market trends and adjust your pricing accordingly.

- **Create Detailed Listings:** When listing sneakers for sale, provide detailed descriptions and high-quality photos. Highlight the condition, size, and any unique features to attract potential buyers.

- **Promote Your Listings:** Use social media, sneaker communities, and online forums to promote your listings. Effective promotion increases visibility and can lead to quicker sales.

Strategic selling practices help you achieve better results and maximize the value of your rare sneakers.

The Impact of Sneaker Culture on Auctions and Releases

Sneaker culture influences the dynamics of auctions and rare releases, shaping market trends and consumer behavior:

- **Increased Demand:** The popularity of sneaker culture has driven demand for rare and exclusive releases, leading to higher prices and competitive auctions.

- **Cultural Significance:** Sneakers with cultural significance, such as collaborations with celebrities or iconic designs, often command higher prices and attract more attention at auctions and releases.

- **Resale Market Influence:** The resale market plays a significant role in determining the value of rare sneakers. Trends and market fluctuations can impact the availability and pricing of coveted pairs.

Understanding the impact of sneaker culture helps you navigate the market and make informed decisions in auctions and rare releases.

Navigating the World of Rare Sneakers

Participating in sneaker auctions and accessing rare releases can be both exciting and challenging. By understanding auction processes, improving your chances of securing rare releases, managing high-value transactions, and leveraging resale marketplaces, you can successfully navigate this high-stakes aspect of sneaker culture.

With the knowledge gained from these chapters, you are well-equipped to handle the complexities of sneaker auctions and rare releases, ensuring a rewarding experience in the world of high-value sneakers. Don't forget to always check out the shipping price before you purchase. Nothing worse than thinking you got

Chapter 12

a sweet deal only to realize your paying a crazy amount for shipping and the deal ends up being no deal at all.

Exploration of sneaker auctions and rare releases, providing strategies and insights for navigating high-stakes transactions.

Sneaker Hustle: The Ultimate Guide to Collecting, Buying, and Selling Sneakers has taken you on a journey through the fast-paced, exciting world of sneaker culture. From understanding the history and evolution of sneaker collecting to learning how to spot fakes, secure rare releases, and succeed in the resale market, you've gained essential tools to thrive as a sneaker enthusiast or entrepreneur.

At its core, the sneaker hustle is about more than just shoes it's about passion, community, and opportunity. Whether you're in it for the love of the game, the thrill of the hunt, or as a business venture, this guide has provided the foundational knowledge needed to navigate the sneaker world with confidence.

Remember, patience, research, and attention to detail are key. Stay informed about market trends, release dates, and new innovations in sneaker technology. Build your collection carefully, sell strategically, and always aim for authenticity and quality.

As sneaker culture continues to grow and evolve, so will the opportunities within it. By staying dedicated, flexible, and knowledgeable, you're set to turn your passion for sneakers into a lasting successful business. The American Dream, doing something you love and making money with it.

Good luck on your sneaker journey and may you always find the perfect pair!

.

www.ingramcontent.com/pod-product-compliance
Lightning Source LLC
Chambersburg PA
CBHW070356230526
45471CB00006B/2593